Presented To:

Presented By:

Date:

from a
Mother's
Heart
to her
Son

NELSON BOOKS
A Division of Thomas Nelson Publishers
Since 1798

www.thomasnelson.com

Published in Nashville, Tennessee, by Thomas Nelson, Inc.

Nelson Books titles may be purchased in bulk for educational, business, fund-raising, or sales promotional use. For information, please e-mail SpecialMarkets@ThomasNelson.com.

Scripture quotations noted NKJV are from The New King James Version®. Copyright © 1979, 1980, 1982 by Thomas Nelson, Inc. Used by permission. All rights reserved.

Scripture quotations noted AMP are from The Amplified Bible: Old Testament. Copyright © 1962, 1964 by Zondervan Publishing House (used by permission); and from THE AMPLIFIED NEW TESTAMENT. Copyright © 1958 by the Lockman Foundation (used by permission).

Scripture quotations noted CEV are from The Contemporary English Version. © 1991 by the American Bible Society. Used by permission.

Scripture quotations noted MSG are from The Message. Copyright © by Eugene H. Peterson 1993, 1994, 1995. Used by permission of NavPress Publishing Group.

Scripture quotations noted NCV are from The Holy Bible, New Century Version, copyright © 1987, 1988, 1991 by Word Publishing, a division of Thomas Nelson, Inc. All rights reserved. Used by permission.

Scripture quotations noted NIV are from the Holy Bible: New International Version®. Copyright © 1973, 1978, 1984 by International Bible Society. Used by permission of Zondervan Publishing House. All rights reserved.

Scripture quotations noted NLT are from the Holy Bible, New Living Translation, copyright © 1996. Used by permission of Tyndale House Publishers, Inc., Wheaton, Illinois 60189. All rights reserved.

Scripture quotations noted NRSV are from The New Revised Standard Version of the Bible. Copyright © 1989 by the Division of Christian Education of the National Council of the Churches of Christ in the U.S.A. All rights reserved.

Managing Editor: Lila Empson
Associate Editor: Kyle L. Olund
Manuscript: Sheila Rabe
Design: Whisner Design Group, Tulsa, Oklahoma

ISBN 0-7852-1431-3

Printed in the United States of America

06 07 08 09 QW 5 4 3 2 1

*You're a child of the King; get a
sense of value to yourself.*

John MacArthur

Contents

Introduction

You are a very special man to me, my son,
and I have long admired your capabilities and
your potential. From the earliest time, you
have given me joy and amazement as you
learned and explored and accomplished. It is
my pleasure to have started you on your journey to manhood, and it will continue to be my
pleasure as you step into your future to make
your mark on the world.

   Son, you are part of the next generation of
men. To you will fall the responsibility to lead
and help others, and to contribute to this great
world in which God has put you. God has His
own unique plan for your life, and as you go
down that exciting road, all who love you will
be watching and rooting for your success. May
the words in this book encourage you as you
live your great adventure.

> He who plants
> kindness gathers
> love.
>
> Saint Basil

You bless the godly, O LORD, surrounding them with your shield of love.
Psalm 5:12 NLT

Having you, son, has been a real adventure.

Son, you've always held a special place in my heart.

Having you, son, has been a true adventure of the heart. You melted my heart every time you flew past wearing pajamas and a bathroom towel cape, launching yourself into a career as the world's next superhero. My heart burst with pride when you gave me your first drawing, when your teacher told me what a sweet boy I had, when you ran up to me in a cap and gown, diploma in hand. And my heart broke over your every sorrow. As you strike out to make your own life, my heart will go with you. And I like to think you'll leave behind a little of your heart. You are my joy, my comfort, my accomplishment, and always, no matter what your age, my boy.

O wonderful son, that can so astonish a mother!

William Shakespeare

Sons are a heritage from the LORD, children are a reward from him.

Psalm 127:3 NIV

You are a son of God and therefore extremely valuable to Him.

God values you and has a plan for your life.

Like every man, you want to find your place in history, want to make your life count for something. And that is exactly what God wants for you, for He has made you to reflect His image. As one of God's sons, your life has special meaning. Your unique gifts and talents, your sense of humor, your insights, your way of interacting with others and contributing to your world, all make you special in the eyes of your Creator. He rejoices in each new skill you master and every worthwhile project you successfully complete. Your life is a bright piece in the ever-changing kaleidoscope of God's creation, as important to the overall design as any other piece. He has a place and a purpose for you. You matter.

> You're a child of the King; get a sense of value to yourself.
>
> John MacArthur

God created man in his own image, in the image of God he created him; male and female he created them.

Genesis 1:27 NIV

Super self-confidence will grow out of confidence in God.

Trust in God's ability to lead you, and you will stay free of self-doubt.

What gives a man true confidence? Is it his strength, his mental power, his past successes? No. True self-confidence grows out of the knowledge of God's ability to lead and direct. When you know God is with you, you can fight any battle, take any risk. When you know God is leading you, you are able to step out boldly into unknown territory. When your confidence rests on a foundation of trust in God's power, you can be confident in using your gifts and talents. The opinions of others won't sway you, and tales of other men's failures won't scare you away. Understand that you can do whatever God calls you to do, and you will be able to make things happen in your life.

> A man who is intimate with God will never be intimidated by men.
>
> Leonard Ravenhill

I have strength for all things in Christ Who empowers me [I am ready for anything and equal to anything through Him Who infuses inner strength into me; I am self-sufficient in Christ's sufficiency].

Philippians 4:13 AMP

All your great accomplishments will start with prayer.

Your life will be both satisfying and eternally successful if you make prayer a habit.

Many great things are still undone in this world. Will you be doing some of them? Very possibly, if you become a man of prayer. Prayer is both your source of inspiration and your map to keep you on the road to accomplishment. Prayer is what keeps you connected to God; prayer is the one thing that can pull you out of the pit of despair when you hit dark times along the way. Prayer is the warrior's secret weapon, the inventor's genius, the composer's inspiration. It has the power to completely transform a man. And why shouldn't it, considering the fact that it is what connects him to the Creator of the universe? Want to accomplish much? Pray.

Prayer is a summit meeting in the throne room of the universe.

Ralph A. Herring

You, dear friends, must continue to build your lives on the foundation of your holy faith. And continue to pray as you are directed by the Holy Spirit.

Jude 20 NLT

You will get rich faster if you don't try to get rich quick.

When it comes to money management, remember that slow and steady wins the race.

Some words combine well with the word quick: *quick as a wink, quick on the draw, quick to the rescue.* There are two words that don't fit well with this particular adjective, though, and they are *get* and *rich*. Money can be quickly lost and quickly spent, but it can rarely be quickly acquired. In fact, when you hear of someone losing his money, it's often because he got greedy and impatient. Wisdom and patience are still the best fertilizer for growing the money God has entrusted to you. Be a wise money manager, and use both. Save and invest a portion of your earnings regularly. Time will pass faster than you can imagine, and you will soon have a bigger nest egg than you thought possible sooner.

> The one principle that surrounds everything else is that of stewardship; that we are the managers of everything that God has given us.
>
> Larry Burkett

Wealth hastily gotten will dwindle, but those who gather little by little will increase it.

Proverbs 13:11 NRSV

*Go ahead and be a nice guy,
because nice guys finish first.*

*Be the kind of man God can be
proud of, and He will reward you
with a good and meaningful life.*

Whoever started the rumor that nice guys finish last must have been a gangster or a corporate swindler, because that statement is pathetically incorrect. Nice guys finish first in all life's most important races. A nice guy like you can quickly find support in times of need. And he's sure to find the nicest girl—and keep her! A nice guy like you doesn't have to buy favors or friendship. God rewards nice guys with the kind of peace of mind that can only come with a clear conscience. Nobody ever looks at a nice guy with scorn and says, "I don't know how you sleep at night." Want to feel good and smile through the day? Want to sleep at night? Keep on being a nice guy.

> He who plants kindness gathers love.
>
> Saint Basil

You bless the godly, O LORD, surrounding them with your shield of love.

Psalm 5:12 NLT

Your authentic self-confidence will grow out of confidence in God.

You are a son of God and, therefore, extremely valuable to Him.

All your great accomplishments will start with prayer.

One of the wisest investments you can make is in good friends.

Friendship is the one investment you can make that not only holds its value but is also guaranteed to grow in value over time.

You will find them everywhere—on TV, on the radio, in the bookstore—investment experts, telling you how to make your life better and more secure. Much of what they tell you will be good, sound advice. But as you go through life, don't forget to invest in more than real estate, gold, and stocks and bonds, because money alone won't bring you loyalty or moral support in times of trouble. For that you need real wealth: friends. When you invest energy in your friendships, you receive a double bonus. You get great times now, and you also build a support team for the future. Be there for your friends now. Build those relationships. The bonds you form will pay dividends all your life.

> No man is a failure who has friends.
>
> Frank Capra

A friend loves at all times, and a brother is born for adversity.

Proverbs 17:17 NKJV

When you master your temper,
you master the world.

It is always easier to prevent problems
by controlling your temper than to do
damage control after you've lost it.

Loss of temper has been known to sabotage many a good man. It can escalate differences into all-out fights and problems into disaster. It can raise blood pressure and ruin dinners. An out-of-control temper can cost a man his friends, his job, even his health. But when a guy can control his temper, look out, world. Be that guy, and you won't waste valuable energy on destructive behavior. Instead, you'll focus your energies on problem solving. You'll already be climbing the mountain while your temperamental counterpart is still shaking his fist at it. You can control any situation once you can control yourself. People will turn to you in an emergency because you keep your cool. Always remember, the man who tames his temper tames his life.

> Self-control is the mother of spiritual health.
>
> Saint John Climacus

My dear brothers and sisters, always be willing to listen and slow to speak. Do not become angry easily, because anger will not help you live the right kind of life God wants.

James 1:19–20 NCV

The best way to start your Monday
is with church on Sunday.

It's a good thing to make church an
important part of your life.

Some people think a guy's week begins on Monday, but it really starts on Sunday. When you go to church on Sunday you set the tone for the rest of the week. Giving that time to your Creator, to worship and learn, sets your priorities in your mind, reminding you that God comes first in your life. That Sunday time spent in God's presence with other believers heals the bruises from the week before. It encourages you and raises your spirits. You get refreshed, renewed, and reminded that you are a son of God, here for a purpose. You may enter God's presence feeling tired and beaten, but you will always leave energized and filled with hope. Surely there's no better way to begin the week.

> He cannot have God for his father who has not the church for his mother.
>
> Saint Cyprian

Some people have gotten out of the habit of meeting for worship, but we must not do that. We should keep on encouraging each other, especially since you know that the day of the Lord's coming is getting closer.

Hebrews 10:25 CEV

Live your life as an open book, and others will find it a great read.

Always remember that people are watching you, and live in a way that brings honor to God.

The best way to live your life is as if it were
the proverbial open book that any passerby
could peruse. You can make it a real page-
turner, filled with humor and adventure. And,
since you're the hero of the story, you'll want
to live like a hero, bravely and honorably, trusting God to deliver you from dark moments
and to strengthen you to resist dark behavior.
If you can live each day in that open book,
you'll not only avoid moral pitfalls, you'll also
create an inspiring life worthy of emulation and
a witness for God worthy of your character. An
open book means that any page can stand up
to scrutiny. What a satisfying accomplishment
to be able to say that about your life!

A good life is the
best sermon.

Author Unknown

Don't hide your light under a basket! Instead,
put it on a stand and let it shine for all.

Matthew 5:15–16 NLT

*The secret to success lies in realizing that
real men admit their mistakes.*

*Always be brave enough to
admit when you're wrong;
people will respect you for it.*

Why should a guy admit when he's wrong? It's a sign of weakness, right? It gives people the upper hand, makes them think that you're a doormat and that they can walk all over you. Not really. The ability to admit when you're wrong can make you likable and a whole lot easier to work with than the guy who's always right even when he's wrong. You want this ability in your social-skills toolbox for sure because it's a great tool for learning and for building friendships. People tolerate the guy who always has to be right, but they genuinely like and want to help the guy who will admit to being human. So go ahead, son, be human. You'll find that you have lots of company.

> There is nothing progressive about being pig-headed and refusing to admit a mistake.
>
> C. S. Lewis

Fools think their own way is right, but the wise listen to advice.

Proverbs 12:15 NRSV

In everything you do, remember
that perseverance not only pays off
but also gives bonuses.

If you keep trying, the day will
come when you'll be glad you did.

Perseverance is a behavior well worth culti-
vating. It builds character. It also garners support. After all, who doesn't admire and want to
help a man who's trying hard to reach a worthwhile goal? Perseverance is sure to increase
your chances of success. The more you try, the
more you learn; and the more you learn, the
better you get and the closer you come to
reaching your goals. That eventual success
brings with it myriad bonuses. You could earn
a raise at work, master a new skill, win a gold
medal or a place on the team, or win the love
of a good woman. One bonus you're guaranteed, and that's the good character and self-
esteem that go to the man who keeps trying.

To persevere is
to succeed.

Thomas Sutcliffe
Mort

Perseverance must finish its work so that you may
be mature and complete, not lacking anything.

James 1:4 NIV

One of the wisest investments you can
make is in good friends.

In everything you do, remember that
perseverance not only pays off
but also gives bonuses.

Live your life as an open book, and
others will find it a great read.

*The more generous you are,
the richer you get.*

*Maintain a giving attitude, and your life
will be rich in all the ways that count.*

Many people believe that the more money they have, the richer they'll be. More money can mean more possessions and more leisure time, but it doesn't make you truly rich. An increase in fortune may buy you lots of good-time buds and a false sense of security, but it can't buy real friends or lasting peace of mind. And it certainly can't buy character. True wealth is, paradoxically, found when you give rather than acquire. When you are generous with what God has given you, you gain the kind of self-respect no amount of money can buy. You spread goodness in a world desperately needy for it and reap the reward of satisfaction and a good name. That kind of wealth will last you a lifetime.

It is in giving that we receive.

Saint Francis of Assisi

Give, and you will receive. You will be given much. Pressed down, shaken together, and running over, it will spill into your lap. The way you give to others is the way God will give to you.

Luke 6:38 NCV

The perfect way to reduce stress is to give your problems to God.

When you are trusting God, there's no need to worry.

The state of the world, the state of the environment, the state of your checkbook— modern-day life will present you with all kinds of problems and dilemmas, all designed to stress you out. But God specializes in stress relief. He isn't overwhelmed by the state of the world, the environment, or your checkbook. He can work out the toughest of problems and help you manage seemingly impossible situations. Nothing overwhelms Him, and nothing you need is beyond Him. If you want to avoid stress, give your worries to God. Tell Him your problems, ask for wisdom, then take a deep breath and relax. There's no need to feel stressed once you put God in control.

Pray and let God worry.

Martin Luther

Cast all your anxiety on him, because he cares for you.

1 Peter 5:7 NRSV

41

Mother's Day is any day you
spend time on your mom.

The best way you show me you love me is
by making time for me in your life.

On some level, we mothers understand that our sons must eventually get lives of their own, with their own friends and activities. We get that. Really. Still, there's that corner of the heart that protests, "But he's important to me. I don't want to lose him. I watched him take his first steps as a child. I want to watch him take all those big-life steps as a man." In other words, we don't want to be forgotten. No matter what your age, you'll always be important to me, and I love spending time with you. Allowing me to share in all the stages of your life is the best present you'll ever give me. Flowers and cards are nice, but my favorite present will always be you.

> Enjoy one another and take the time to enjoy family life together.
>
> Billy Graham

Listen to your father who begot you, and do not despise your mother when she is old.

Proverbs 23:22 NKJV

When you have both passion and integrity, women will find you irresistible.

The best way for you to be the kind of man a woman wants is to be the kind of man she can admire.

I know women can be hard to understand, so let me tell you what they want. Every red-blooded girl dreams about meeting a romantic and passionate man who will sweep her off her feet Prince Charming style. And she dreams about more than that. She imagines that first kiss when Mr. Wonderful will make her see stars—with her eyes closed! What she doesn't want to dream about or even consider is the possibility of finding a frog hiding behind that princely guise. No woman wants a man who has more charm than character and who considers her heart disposable. I'm confident that you'll always be a prince of a guy where women are concerned and will treat them with respect. Do that and you won't be sorry, because while charm may interest a woman, it's character that will keep her.

> The most precious possession that ever comes to a man in this world is a woman's heart.
>
> Josiah G. Holland

Whoever tries to live right and be loyal finds life, success, and honor.

Proverbs 21:21 NCV

You're a winner when you don't let losing defeat you.

Keep a winning attitude, and you will have a winning life.

That moment when the horn blows and the game ends can be painful when you're on the losing team. But those moments of loss and victory are equally short. After the end-of-game high fives, the fans go home. The season ends, and a new round of competition begins. That's why you can shake off your losses and set your sights on the next challenge, because losing is a temporary situation. Whether you fumble the ball or fumble an opportunity at work, keep in mind, that mistake is only one small moment in a very long game. Keep praying and keep playing, and remember that the biggest difference between winners and losers is their attitude. Keep a winner's hang-in-there attitude, and don't get discouraged. Your big win could be right around the corner.

The greatest test of courage on earth is to bear defeat without losing courage.

Robert G. Ingersoll

We know that all things work together for good for those who love God, who are called according to his purpose.

Romans 8:28 NRSV

The way you have good relationships is by having godly ones.

Honor God in all your relationships, and you will make Him, others, and yourself happy.

Relationships are a lot like a car; they run best when you maintain them. Of course, you know that if you want an engine to purr, you have to give it oil. It's the same with people. You want to treat them the way you'd treat the car of your dreams: do all that needs to be done to keep everything in good running order. God has designed relationships to run on love, kindness, and consideration. Son, I know you want your relationships to be good ones, so I'm confident you'll be honest, kind, and considerate with the people you care about. And you won't be sorry. Maintaining those relationships with God's love will keep them running smoothly, no matter how many miles you put on them.

A man's feeling of good will toward others is the strongest magnet for drawing good will from others.

Lord Philip Dormer
Stanhope
Chesterfield

Love is kind and patient, never jealous, boastful, proud, or rude. Love isn't selfish or quick tempered. It doesn't keep a record of wrongs that others do. Love rejoices in the truth, but not in evil.

1 Corinthians 13:4–6 CEV

The way you have good relationships
is by having godly ones.

You're a winner when you don't
let losing defeat you.

When you are truly generous,
you will become truly rich.

Today is a great day for you to take time to be happy.

Find something to enjoy every day, and you will have a happy life.

There are some things a guy just shouldn't put off, and being happy is one of them. Why wait until every goal is reached and every mountain climbed to enjoy your life? As the saying goes, it's not the destination; it's the journey. As you move toward achieving your life goals, take time to appreciate the friends, the interesting experiences, and the memories you're collecting along the way. Savor the moments of shared laughter. Appreciate the sunrises and sunsets of each day. On your way to the mountaintop, stop and take a picture of the waterfall. God fills every day of a man's life with good things. Take time to appreciate and enjoy those small moments because, added together, they are the gems that make life so priceless.

> There is not one blade of grass, there is no color in this world that is not intended to make us rejoice.
>
> John Calvin

This is the day that the LORD has made.
Let us rejoice and be glad today!

Psalm 118:24 NCV

Be stubborn when it really matters,
and concede when it doesn't.

Be willing to meet others halfway—
you don't have to be "right"
every time.

It's not always a bad thing to be stubborn. You should never cave when important moral issues are at stake. But sometimes giving in is a good idea. Whether you're in a committee meeting or a business meeting, being open to trying someone else's ideas may earn you more cooperation than obstinate insistence on the other person's choosing your way or the highway. When you don't have to win every argument or always have your way, you show maturity and make being around you an experience people want to repeat. You gain respect, and people often become more willing to meet you halfway and compromise. Some things really can't be negotiated, but some things can. Be a wise son, and learn to distinguish between the two.

> The aim of an argument or discussion should not be victory but progress.
>
> Joseph Joubert

Foolish people are always fighting, but avoiding quarrels will bring you honor.

Proverbs 20:3 NCV

Giving in to impulses to do good will make you feel great.

Be open to instant inspiration and off-the-cuff kindness, and who knows what adventures you'll have.

Impulsiveness is generally considered a bad behavior. You often hear it linked with spending mistakes or foolish actions that lead to trouble. But impulsiveness can be good when you marry it to kindness. The person you help benefits, and so do you. Stop to help a woman stuck in traffic with a flat tire, and you can drive off feeling like the Lone Ranger. *Who was that masked man?* Shovel snow off the walk for an elderly neighbor, and you'll go home feeling warm all over. Slip a little money to someone in need, and you'll encourage that person and make yourself feel great at the same time. Doing things on the spur of the moment can be fun and exciting. Doing good things for others will be all that, and fulfilling, too.

> Do all the good you can, by all the means you can, in all the ways you can, at all the times you can, as long as ever you can.
>
> John Wesley

As we have opportunity, let us do good to all, especially to those who are of the household of faith.

Galatians 6:10 NKJV

Obstacles are only hurdles waiting for you to jump over them.

Look at your problems as opportunities for growth, and you'll find it easier to overcome them.

Son, have you ever wondered why you so often encounter obstacles when you're trying to reach a goal? Why can't you simply achieve it without some problem popping up to complicate matters? Maybe because such an easy accomplishment would have little value. Every hero needs obstacles. They are what prove he's a hero. The more he overcomes, the stronger he gets. And the more his skills and determination are tested, the sweeter his success. Don't despair when you find obstacles on your path to success. They're only hurdles, not dead ends. They'll make your personal race exciting, and you'll learn and grow from the challenges. Find a way around those obstacles, and, while you're looking, think how sweet your success will taste when you finally achieve your goal. And remember, I'm always rooting for you!

Little minds are tamed and subdued by misfortunes; but great minds rise above them.

Washington Irving

My brethren, count it all joy when you fall into various trials, knowing that the testing of your faith produces patience.

James 1:2–3 NKJV

The best way for you to even the score is to give God the scorecard.

There is never a need for revenge, because you have more important things to do with your life.

There are times when it's good to keep score, like during a football game. Then there are times when it's counterproductive, as in real life. Still, some sons think they need to do just that. When someone hurts or offends them, they promise themselves, "I'll get that guy." But when you trust God with your life, you don't have to waste energy and brainpower on that sort of thing. He will take care of the other guy just fine. If someone does something bad to you, shake it off. You needn't concern yourself with evening the score. God can take care of that. Focus instead on your own game and your own goal. If you do, you'll make good yardage in life.

The only people with whom you should try to get revenge are those who have helped you.

John E. Sutherland

Beloved, never avenge yourselves, but leave the way open for [God's] wrath; for it is written, Vengeance is Mine, I will repay (requite), says the Lord.

Romans 12:19 AMP

When you show courage and take difficult steps, God will keep you from falling.

Whether you're taking a stand or taking a chance, God will be with you.

You may be called to do things in life that make you feel like you're facing a rope bridge spanning a jungle ravine. You look at it and think, *Do I dare step on this? Will it hold me? Is it too late to turn back?* It takes courage to step past your doubt and fear and start walking, trusting that you're right where God wants you. It takes courage to commit to the journey, to make moral stands that may not be popular, to take risks that look foolish to your family and friends, to move out of your comfort zone into new, uncharted territory. If you just lift your foot and take that step of faith, God will guide you. He'll get you safely over the ravine.

> Better, though difficult, the right way to go, than wrong, though easy, where the end is woe.
>
> John Bunyan

I, the LORD your God, hold your right hand; it is I who say to you, "Do not fear, I will help you."

Isaiah 41:13 NRSV

Be stubborn when it really matters,
and concede when it doesn't.

Obstacles are only hurdles waiting
for you to jump over them.

Today is a great day for you
to take time to be happy.

When you manage your money well, you manage your life well, too.

Always remember that ultimately, it isn't money that makes things possible in your life, but you, because you are the one who manages your money.

Money. Some people say it makes the world go around; others claim it's evil. Most people complain that they don't have enough of it. What is it, really? Nothing more than a tool. If you manage it wisely, you can build good things into your life, things like security and the opportunity to invest in yourself and others and to partner with good causes. What's the secret of good money management? Make sure you love people and use money rather than the other way around. Budget wisely and give generously, and always give to God first. Save habitually so you'll have money for both future emergencies and future opportunities. And ask God to guide your decisions. He's the world's best financial adviser.

> Money is always either our master or our slave.
>
> Latin Proverb

Wisdom is a shelter as money is a shelter, but the advantage of knowledge is this: that wisdom preserves the life of its possessor.

Ecclesiastes 7:12 NIV

God can take your disappointments and turn them into hope.

The best way to get through the disappointment is to trust that God is leading you into something better.

Sweet as life is, some days can turn a little sour. Your best-laid plans can unravel, and people you trust the most can let you down. Disappointment is a fact of life. But so are comfort and restoration. When you feel that you have a black cloud over your head, remember the rainbow. God is a God of new beginnings and promise. He brings life from a dying seed, spins sunrise out of darkness, and soothes hurting hearts. No matter what you go through, He will be with you, offering comfort and strength and hope for a brighter tomorrow. Life has a way of raining on our parades, but next time it rains on yours, ask God to help you look through the rain and see the rainbow.

You can't appreciate the miracle of sunrise unless you've waited in the darkness.

Author Unknown

You changed my sorrow into dancing. You took away my clothes of sadness, and clothed me in happiness.

Psalm 30:11 NCV

You keep two things when you obey the law: your self-respect and your money.

Always remember that the benefits of keeping the law outweigh any so-called benefits of breaking it.

You will always want to be a law-abiding citizen, because it pleases God. But there are other, more practical reasons why it's good to obey the law. For one thing, you keep your respect. You can look in the mirror and like the guy looking back at you. You can walk down the street with your head held high. Then there's the matter of money. Lawbreaking can get expensive. Fines, court costs—who wants to waste money on them when there are so many better ways to spend it? How many CDs could a man buy for the cost of one fine? How many ball games could he attend? Obey the law, and your bank account will thank you. So will the guy in the mirror.

The ship that will not obey the helm will have to obey the rocks.

English Proverb

Make the Master proud of you by being good citizens. Respect the authorities, whatever their level.

1 Peter 2:13 MSG

Faith is God's power tool to help you build a satisfying life.

Trust God's guidance and act on it, and you will build the best possible life for yourself.

For a project to turn out well, you need the right tools. You especially need the right tools when the project is your life. That is where faith comes in. Faith is confidence in God that grows from a true and close friendship with Him. Faith gives you the inner power to move into new and exciting territory. It sculpts the vision for what can eventually become reality. Faith says, "God is with me. I can go for it." Even a little faith moves mountains and conquers fear and opposition. If you want to build a life of purpose and adventure, let faith be your favorite tool. Believe God's promises and act on them. This will help you blast through obstacles and build the future of your dreams.

A little faith will bring your soul to heaven; a great faith will bring heaven to your soul.

Charles Spurgeon

"Even if you had faith as small as a mustard seed," the Lord answered, "you could say to this mulberry tree, 'May God uproot you and throw you into the sea,' and it would obey you!"

Luke 17:6 NLT

Who you are will always be more than what you do for a living.

God expects you to earn a living, but He also expects you to build a life.

Did you know that in some cultures it's considered rude to make small talk by asking a man what he does for a living? How smart! Those people understand that there's more to a man than how he earns his earthly keep. Hopefully, you do too, and you see yourself first as a child of God. You are here to experience the life He gave you. Of course, you'll want to do well in your career. It would be tragic if you didn't. But it would be equally tragic if your definition of self ever became tied to that alone. You have unique skills and dreams. And throughout your life you'll have many hobbies and interests. Always remember, no matter how many hours of your day a job requires, it's a small part of who you are.

> Vocation does not give identity.
>
> Anthony Campolo

What profit remains for the worker from his toil?

Ecclesiastes 3:9 AMP

Break any bad habit the same way you climb a mountain: one step at a time.

Concentrate on winning over unwanted habits hour by hour and day by day, and you will eventually conquer them.

Bad habits can get in the way of a good life. They're like gum on a shoe: easy to pick up, hard to get off. In fact, bad habits can cling so stubbornly that just thinking about breaking one can make a man decide to file that idea under "tomorrow." But anything that can be picked up can also be put down, so if you acquire a habit you want to lose, don't despair. You can lose it the same way you'd climb a mountain: one step at a time. Break that challenging journey into small stages, and you can beat any habit. Bad habits may not leave as quickly as they came, but if you keep working to shed them, they eventually get the idea they're not wanted.

> The best way to break a habit is to drop it.
>
> H. S. Yoder

In everything we have won more than a victory because of Christ who loves us.

Romans 8:37 CEV

Thinking before you speak is like using your car brakes: you prevent serious damage.

If you consider your words before speaking, you'll not only avoid many misunderstandings, but you'll also help heal hurts and make the world a better place.

What do a guy's mouth and his car have in common? Both can do a lot of damage. Words are powerful, and when you speak thoughtlessly or in anger, your words can have a devastating impact on another person. When your mouth starts moving, you're the one behind the wheel. You're the one who controls what you say. You can direct where a conversation goes. You can stop yourself from saying hurtful things. You can even say things that will head off a verbal collision. Keeping that in mind, consider carefully before you speak. Your words may be a powerful vehicle, but your mind gives you power brakes, and you can use those brakes whenever you feel a conversation skidding out of control.

> Wisdom is knowing when to speak your mind and when to mind your speech.
>
> Author Unknown

Those who are careful about what they say protect their lives, but whoever speaks without thinking will be ruined.

Proverbs 13:3 NCV

When you manage your money well,
you manage your life well too.

You keep two things when you obey the
law: your self-respect and your money.

Who you are will always be more
than what you do for a living.

An attitude of gratitude changes your outlook, your day, and your life.

Appreciating every day of your life is the secret to being happy with your life.

Going through each day with a "gratitude attitude" can't help but give you a good life, because that grateful perspective will allow you to see things differently. Instead of looking at what's wrong and feeling miserable, you'll be able to focus on what's right and feel good. The more you look for what's right in your life, the better your vision will get and the more you'll see. And the more you see, the happier you'll be. And that I've-got-it-good kind of happiness will turn you into a human magnet, attracting good people and great opportunities. (After all, who doesn't want to help a guy who's easy to please?) Remember to be grateful for the good things in your life, son, and you'll soon find them multiplying.

A life of thankfulness releases the glory of God.

Bengt Sundberg

In everything give thanks; for this is the will of God in Christ Jesus for you.

1 Thessalonians 5:18 NKJV

Be good at small things, and you will soon be great at big things.

The seeds of greatness can grow even in the humblest of places.

Ah, the exciting opportunities life is waiting to present you! Who knows what you will accomplish, what mountaintop you'll hit, what pinnacles of success you'll scale. Remember, though, as you eye that exciting place at the top, no one begins his journey there. The greatest men in history marched their way to greatness from a base camp of humility, tackling small assignments and then moving on to increasingly more difficult challenges and positions of responsibility. Follow in their steps, and be faithful in whatever responsibility you're given, no matter how small. Don't scorn seemingly insignificant jobs or humble positions. Instead, see them as stepping-stones to greater opportunities. Learn, work, achieve. This simple formula will give you satisfaction wherever you are and lead you to all kinds of opportunities.

> He is truly great who is little in his own eyes and makes nothing of the highest honor.
>
> Thomas à Kempis

He said, "Good servant! Great work! Because you've been trustworthy in this small job, I'm making you governor of ten towns."

Luke 19:17 MSG

God always has a reward waiting for you at the end of a trial.

Every hard thing you will ever go through has both a purpose for your life and a reward waiting on the other side.

You're bound to face times when you feel like Steven Spielberg could make a movie of your life and call it *Job, the Next Generation.* But the good news is that God loves a happy ending as much as anyone. Even more, in fact, since He is the original Creator of happy endings. He loves to take sons from slavery to positions of power, to reward the suffering faithful with relief, and to bring resurrection out of death. Heaven and eternal life are His gifts to man. So when you're feeling like Job, comfort yourself with the sure knowledge that God is on your side. Hang in there, and, like Job, you will find God's reward waiting at the end of your trials and tribulations.

The trials of the saints are a "divine pruning," by which he grows and brings forth abundant fruit.

C. H. Spurgeon

Blessed is the man who perseveres under trial, because when he has stood the test, he will receive the crown of life that God has promised to those who love him.

James 1:12 NIV

For those important life questions, older people are the best encyclopedia you can consult.

When you take advantage of the wisdom of the older generation, you gain knowledge.

How do I splice a severed electrical cord back together? How much of my paycheck should I invest, and where? How do I fill out this tax form? As you prepare to set out on your own, you can find yourself stumped by all kinds of life details. And that's where the older generation comes in handy. They've been around a lot longer than you, and have learned the business of life. They can tell the difference between a great deal and a rip-off, an opportunity and a misstep. They can tell you how to fix a leaky sink or a shaky relationship. They've witnessed a chunk of history and have learned about human behavior. And they want to help you succeed in life. Borrow from their wisdom, and you'll get smart fast.

Learn all you can from older people. They've been down the road you must travel.

Author Unknown

My son, pay attention to my wisdom;
listen carefully to my wise counsel.

Proverbs 5:1 NLT

As you go through life, you'll find that honesty is the only way to travel.

Be honest and aboveboard in all your dealings, and you will be safe from the trouble that dogs the dishonest man.

Being honest in your dealings is a great safety measure. It can keep you out of hot water, help you avoid moral pitfalls, and steer you clear of the slippery slope that leads to ruin and disgrace. Any situation will be more easily assessed when you are honest with yourself and others. Family and friends will support and invest in your endeavors because they can trust you not to cheat them. Honesty will steer you clear of the kind of shady business dealings that lead to scandals, trials, and ugly headlines. Honesty will make your relationships with others genuine and will allow you to genuinely like yourself. Honesty attracts true friendship and makes the road of life a much safer and happier one. It is truly the best policy.

> Honesty prospers in every condition of life.
>
> Johann Friedrich Von Schiller

My mouth speaks what is true, for my lips detest wickedness.

Proverbs 8:7 NIV

It's okay to fail, because failure is really guidance in disguise.

*Never let failure defeat you.
Instead, let it teach you.*

Failure is a word that often gets a bum rap, as if the worst thing that can happen to a man is to fail. But failure in and of itself is not a bad thing. (How can it be bad to fail when it means you at least tried?) Failure can mean you haven't yet found the right method or formula. It may mean you need to get more training or go back to the drawing board. It may even mean you're ahead of your time. Try to see your failures as God's guidance counselors helping you figure out what to do with yourself. Never stamp "The End" on a failure. Instead, consider it a springboard for a new beginning. God may have something better right around the corner.

> Men's best successes come after their disappointments.
>
> Henry Ward Beecher

Be strong and do not give up, for your work will be rewarded.

2 Chronicles 15:7 NIV

An attitude of gratitude changes your outlook, your day, and your life.

Your first step to doing great things is to be faithful in doing small things.

God always has a reward waiting for you at the end of a trial.

If you can be patient with others' faults, you'll all be happier.

The best way to deal with others' faults is to accept them.

Human beings—wouldn't it be great if they could behave as perfectly as God designed them to behave? Even the most perfect people have their faults and irritating habits. You can do nothing to fix anyone else's flaws. People will always be people, an interesting mixture of boring and quirky, good and bad, kind and indifferent. The best way to deal with them is to accept them. Do that, and you'll avoid much frustration. Disappointment and anger will find it hard to gain a foothold when you shrug and say, "Oh, well. We're all human." Dealing with people is always easier when you cut them some slack. If you do that, who knows? Maybe when you need a little slack, someone will do the same for you.

> Patience will achieve more than force.
>
> Edmund Burke

We urge you, brothers, warn those who are idle, encourage the timid, help the weak, be patient with everyone.

1 Thessalonians 5:14 NIV

There is one perfect place to have pride, and that is in your work.

You can never regret taking pride in your work and doing your very best.

Pride is the polish that makes your work shine. Pride insists on doing the best job possible because your reputation is on the line. That attitude benefits many people. The person who buys your service or product gets something excellent that he can appreciate. That person's satisfaction in turn benefits your company by giving it a good name. When the company does well, all its employees can rest assured they will be able to pay the bills. Artists aren't the only ones who sign their work. Every man leaves his mark on what he does. Your work will show you to be either careless and lazy or dedicated and responsible. Pride yourself on your good work, and you'll create something good for both yourself and others.

Every job is a self-portrait of the person who did it. Autograph your work with excellence.

Author Unknown

Work hard and cheerfully at whatever you do, as though you were working for the Lord rather than for people.

Colossians 3:23 NLT

*Responsibility is God's vote
of confidence in you.*

*Make the most of the responsibilities
God gives you because He's giving
them to you for a reason.*

Some guys think it's a terrible thing to be tied down with responsibilities, but they've got it all wrong. Responsibility isn't a punishment. Responsibility is an honor given to the man gifted and mature enough to handle it, one that brings its own unique rewards. Be thankful for each new responsibility God entrusts to you, because with each one He is saying, "Here is a man I know can handle this. Here is someone who is no longer a child content to hang around the playground. Here is a man ready to face the world." Whenever responsibility settles on your shoulders, see yourself as honored rather than burdened, promoted rather than tied down. God has every confidence that, with His help, you can do what He calls you to do.

> Responsibility is the price of greatness.
>
> Winston Churchill

The LORD God took the man and put him in the garden of Eden to till it and keep it.

Genesis 2:15 NRSV

Forgiveness is the best glue you'll ever find to hold people together.

Make forgiveness a lifestyle, and you will be doing a lot to make your world a better place.

Strive to practice forgiveness, because this is a society that needs it desperately. With people busy nursing grudges and feeding on anger, your forgiveness can become an emotional Red Cross, helping to rebuild broken relationships in the wake of disaster. Anger divides, but forgiveness unites. Not only will the people to whom you extend forgiveness benefit, but you will, too. Your stress levels will go down and your health will be better, and so will your outlook on life. Relationships will be easier, too, because forgiveness is the soothing oil that enables people to work together. Most important, an opportunity to forgive is an opportunity to be like Christ. If for no other reason than that, forgive.

Forgiveness is God's command.

Martin Luther

Be gentle with one another, sensitive. Forgive one another as quickly and thoroughly as God in Christ forgave you.

Ephesians 4:32 MSG

Don't waste your time boasting, because God loves to promote the humble man.

Live a life that pleases God and do great things for him, and He will put you exactly where you need to be.

Humility is a very underrated character quality in Western culture. Instead, an inflated level of self-esteem coupled with shameless self-promotion make up the touted formula for success. "After all, if you don't sell yourself, who will?" say the success gurus. "Blow your own horn; make your own success." But a little horn-blowing goes a long way. Pretty soon when Harry Horn Blower enters a room, everyone scatters. You don't need to boast, because God can spotlight your achievements much more efficiently than you ever could. You don't need to push your way into being somebody, because you'll be somebody simply by being who God has called you to be. Stay humble. That is the kind of son God can use. That is the kind of son He will raise to greatness.

> The first test of a really great man is his humility.
>
> John Ruskin

Whoever exalts himself [with haughtiness and empty pride] shall be humbled (brought low), and whoever humbles himself [whoever has a modest opinion of himself and behaves accordingly] shall be raised to honor.

Matthew 23:12 AMP

When you put God first, all other priorities take care of themselves.

When you put God above everything else, He will make sure you accomplish everything you need to accomplish.

Life's priorities were easy to identify when you were a child, weren't they? Come home from school and play, or go to practice and hope Coach noticed how much you'd improved since the week before. Other things like chores and eating your vegetables didn't show up on your radar. In fact, very little showed up at all, so priorities weren't a problem. Then you got older, and new priorities competed for your attention: girls, jobs, meetings, league play-offs. Now life is so busy it may seem like a puzzle with pieces that multiply when you're not looking. The key to putting it all together is that most important piece: your relationship with God. Put that in place first, and everything else in your life will fall into place and make sense.

> There is no true love to God which is not habitually supreme.
>
> Edward Griffin

Love the LORD your God with all your heart, soul, and strength.

Deuteronomy 6:5 CEV

There is one perfect place to have pride,
and that is in your work.

You don't need to bother with boasting,
because God loves to promote the humble man.

Responsibility is God's vote
of confidence in you.

The best way you can gain others' respect is to respect them first.

Always treat others with the same respect you desire.

Here's a riddle for you. What is something every man wants but never gets unless he gives it first? You're right. It's respect. Respect is impossible to command. You may demand and get an outward show of it, but you can't force it into anyone's heart. It must be inspired rather than enforced. How do you inspire it? Take a lesson from your mirror. A mirror reflects what you give it. Smile, and your mirror image smiles. Tell him he's great, and he returns the compliment. This same principle applies to people. People will perceive you as you perceive them. See them as God's creation and treat them accordingly, and they will do the same for you. So, the next time you want some respect, remember the mirror.

> He that respects not is not respected.
>
> George Herbert

Pay all that you owe, whether it is taxes
and fees or respect and honor.

Romans 13:7 CEV

If you want to be wise, see every experience as a learning opportunity.

Whether they're good or bad, you can learn from every experience and come out better.

"Chalk it up to experience." "Experience is the best teacher." What do these sayings mean, really? God is the ultimate teacher, and life is the best school of all. If you're open to learning as you live, you'll learn patience from frustrating situations, compassion from exposure to suffering, and diplomacy from dealing with difficult people. A wrong bus or a missed flight, a brain-breaking assignment, getting fired, getting the chance of a lifetime, getting exposed to a new way of thinking—anything can turn out to be great insight into human nature. So look for opportunities in unusual places, and you'll get an advanced degree in wise living.

> Nothing is a waste of time if you use the experience wisely.
>
> Auguste Rodin

Teach the wise, and they will become even wiser; teach good people, and they will learn even more.

Proverbs 9:9 NCV

You'll find the secret of success hiding behind the words "hard work."

Success is waiting for you, so don't be afraid to put in the effort you need in order to achieve it.

Wouldn't it be nice if success were like microwave popcorn? A couple of minutes, and voilá, you'd have success! But success isn't instant. Remember, son, most great men of history, captains of industry, and business tycoons got where they did by lots of hard work. Where you find *success*—financial, social, physical, academic, spiritual, and more—will depend on what's important to you. Don't worry if you seem to have to work awfully hard for those material (or tangible) things you need to live. That's the way it goes sometimes. And don't forget to put time and effort into those areas of your life that carry lasting value—love, peace of mind, health, family. Your hard work is the vehicle that can lead you down the road to success.

> Genius begins great works; labor alone finishes them.
>
> Joseph Joubert

Lazy people want much but get little, but those who work hard will prosper and be satisfied.

Proverbs 13:4 NLT

A positive attitude makes you
happier and every day easier.

You will never regret developing
and maintaining a positive attitude.

It's often been said there are two kinds of people: the ones who go to a picnic and see the great food and the ones who go and see only the ants. Guess which person has a better time? Looking at things in a positive way always improves your life. It makes you happier, and your happiness affects your behavior in a positive way, which, in turn, makes the people you're around happy too. Pretty soon, no one is seeing the ants at the picnic. They're all too busy admiring the blue sky and enjoying the potato salad and another's company. A positive attitude can keep you smiling. It will make conversation more pleasant and a hard day easier. A good attitude is the key to a good life.

> The way you see life will largely determine what you get out of it.
>
> Zig Ziglar

If you are cheerful, you feel good; if you are sad, you hurt all over.

Proverbs 17:22 CEV

Be the best you can be, and you'll have the best possible life.

The way to make your life both productive and happy is to concentrate on doing your best and to let God decide the rest.

This is a culture where everyone wants to be the best at something. People compete for all kinds of titles and championships in order to make their lives matter. Life becomes a race with too may people trying for too few prizes. But really, your life is more like a golf game where the most important person you'll ever compete against is yourself. Never waste energy worrying about how your game stacks up against anyone else's. Just concentrate on improving your own game. Instead of striving to be the best, focus on doing your best. By doing that, you'll find enjoyment as well as accomplishment. You'll be satisfied not only with what you've accomplished, but also with the knowledge that you did your best.

> If a man does his best, what else is there?
>
> General
> George S. Patton

Let every person carefully scrutinize and examine and test his own conduct and his own work. He can then have the personal satisfaction and joy of doing something commendable [in itself alone] without [resorting to] boastful comparison with his neighbor.

Galatians 6:4 AMP

119

Be a true hero, and stay true to your beliefs in all circumstances.

God made you to be a hero, so stay true to what you know to be right.

In books and movies, what's the difference between a hero and a villain? Character. The villain may start out good, but he ultimately proves himself too weak to hold on to his beliefs, and down he falls into the murky depths. The hero, on the other hand, ignores the siren song of bad influences and holds tightly to his principles and emerges with the big red *S* still on his chest. Like all heroes, you will be faced with many choices in your life. Be the hero you were called to be, and make the right choice. Sometimes the cost will be great, but never mind, because it will be nothing compared to the priceless reward of self-respect and eternal acclaim that you'll earn at the end of your story.

> We need to set our course by the stars and not by the lights of every passing ship.
>
> Omar Bradley

Do not, therefore, fling away your fearless confidence, for it carries a great and glorious compensation.

Hebrews 10:35 AMP

Hold true to the vision God has placed in your heart, and watch good things happen.

Never settle for anything less than what you know God has called you to do.

You are a unique package. The vision God has given you for building your life is equally unique. It won't look the same as your family's or your friends', because God has a place just for you, a spot to fill, a purpose to accomplish. Allow Him to work in and through you, using each day, each gift, each talent to build something strong and good and glowing with His touch. Friends may want you to come share their dreams, but if their dreams aren't tied with yours, decline the offer. Family may want you to stay close and safe. (Your mother may especially want this!) But do what you know God wants you to do. Follow the vision He has given you. It will lead to good places.

> Choose now to move forward, positively and confidently into your incredible future.
>
> Author Unknown

There has never been the slightest doubt in my mind that the God who started this great work in you would keep at it and bring it to a flourishing finish on the very day Christ Jesus appears.

Philippians 1:6 MSG

If you want to be wise, see every
experience as a learning opportunity.

You'll find the secret of success hiding
behind the words "hard work."

Be the best you can be, and you'll have
the best possible life.

You're a child of the King; get a sense of value to yourself.

John MacArthur

Don't hide your light under a basket! Instead,
put it on a stand and let it shine for all.

Matthew 5:15–16 NLT